2.00

D1559391

BOTERO'S
BEAUTIFUL
HORSES

also by Jan Conn

Red Shoes in the Rain (1984)
The Fabulous Disguise of Ourselves (1986)
South of the Tudo Bem Café (1990)
What Dante Did with Loss (1994)
Beauties on Mad River (2000)
Jaguar Rain (2006)

BOTERO'S
BEAUTIFUL
HORSES

JAN CONN

For Shar and Redwan—
Hope you'll come and visit!
All my best,
Jan

Brick Books Feb 2010

Library and Archives Canada Cataloguing in Publication

Conn, Jan, 1952–
       Botero's beautiful horses / Jan Conn.

Poems.
Includes bibliographical references.
ISBN 978-1-894078-71-9

I. Title.

PS8555.O543B68 2009   C811'.54   C2009-900379-1

We acknowledge the Canada Council for the Arts, the Government of
Canada through the Book Publishing Industry Development Program
(BPIDP), and the Ontario Arts Council for their support of our
publishing program.

 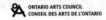

The cover image is "Mexico en negro" by Leslie Zeidenweber.

The author photograph was taken by Mace Neufeld.

The book is set in Minion Pro.

Design and layout by Alan Siu.
Printed and bound by Sunville Printco Inc.

Brick Books
431 Boler Road, Box 20081
London, Ontario N6K 4G6

www.brickbooks.ca

for Carlo

for Diane Conn and Mace Neufeld

"What was pointed out to me was never there; only what was there was there."

—Fernando Pessoa

"All the images of darkness hovered for me in the Mexican sunlight."

—P.K. Page

"—What is the weight of light?"

—Clarice Lispector

"She does not paint time, but the moments when time is resting."

—Octavio Paz (from a poem
about the painter, Remedios Varo)

CONTENTS

The Light of Poinsettias

Cosmological

Blunted Gold

Amazonia

Absolute Love

Harmonium

The Light of Poinsettias

Ahora

Oracular, binocular, what can you see?
—brown metal silhouette of a bull on a hill,
on the hill the broken ahora.

Today, across the top of the temple,
sound of stone boots.

    Then comes the red animal god,

adoration occurring a few km underground.

In the deep canyon below the volcano
little black ribbons of water come and go.

    I will learn to read by the light of poinsettias.

≋

If I ever get to sleep,
    if I ever get to sleep on the Aeroméxico flight

with the joyous Mexican families returning to Tijuana
and the pink-skinned gringos en route to gringolandia

    the luggage lost two weeks
        and the xylophone duet in the zócalo,

headache from the altitude, not the fifth
bottle of Sangre de Toro.

    Below, navy blue mountains and serge plains,
convolutions resembling images of brains

and down the aisle dispersing peanuts and que quieres
para bebir come the Mexican goddesses

 cunningly disguised as stewardesses,

  serpents coiled in their braids.

   ≋

My Mexico City is filled with unusable red

hidden beneath Frida's cobalt walls,
in the shade of casuarina trees,

in a hot humming ball in the lower left
of Siqueiros' mural in the Castillo—

 crimson to earth

carnation to smoke

  lily to dust

  luminous crystal to nothingness.

   ≋

At night the kinkajou climbs down the tree on tiptoe, long tongue first,

and the larger-than-life papier mâché dolls
 perk up, go hustling through the walls

out into the cobbled streets of Coyoacán,

mischievous, playing silly tricks.

Or are they you, awakened
from your spent but passionate slumber,

uneasy, volatile, cigarette
in one hand,

stiffened paintbrush in the other?

≋

Women in white lace
in fields of marigolds and poppies.

A headless god behind glass.

The Angel of the Revolution
painted into a corner.

At Xochicalco a vermillion flycatcher flares among the trees,

the serpents exhale a last smoky breath,
curl at the foot of the temple.

≋

To cross the Isthmus of Tehuantepec
requires a moonlit wooden boat,

Captain Donkey sporting a woven cap.

The sail a white dress shirt.
Atop the broomstick mast, a pink banana flower.

Let us go now, my love, row and row.

≋

Oaxaca in 1795 in Nueva España lies between the Rio Atoyaque
    and the Rio Xalatlaco.

One section of the city is parrot yellow, one
    oxblood, one pale mandarin orange,

the fourth section no colour at all.

One hundred stone masks, blank-eyed, in a field of dark pink lilies.

Half a watermelon, a skeleton perched on a fish.

DH Lawrence strikes for Dorothy Brett a provocative pose
    atop the aqueduct. It's 1924.

A flower in my hair all I ever wanted.

≋

A celestial band of diminutive trumpet flowers
    circles el centro, makes the stones quiver.

Those of us left standing are shaken.

From the church entrance Santo Domingo descends
    headfirst.

The long swim upriver from the Gulf of Mexico
must account for the dazed expression
of the blue-tailed mermaid.

≋

There are two paths to your body. I travel on one, wavering.

The other is dry heat, almost tropical. Along it
        a fifteen-year-old beauty

climbs out of a white jeep, decorously

wends her way among the pillars of the roofless basilica.

        Volcanic cantera in amber and pale green
sucks in the light and emanates it, centuries old, complex,

        dense, framing all our bodies in gold.

≋

New year in Oaxaca, old year too.

Of the seven trees of January, el tule
        is the one I can't lie to,

                overwhelming as Paradise.

≋

Night the blue of armadillo
　　　after the firemen have quenched the stars.

Up on the pitted table she swings a single leg in plaster
and a bottle of something green.

　　The plants in the Botanical Gardens below

　　trade stems, leaves, blossoms
　　　　in the dark.

　　Incandescent in a scarlet suit, the thin architect at his desk
　　　　overlooking the hotel lobby

plots the erratic course of love.

The Flower Carriers

In Chapultepec Park a hundred coffins, followed by weeping widows,
ride on the bronze backs of Botero's beautiful horses.

On some lips El Día de los Muertos is like the taste of honey.

Why we are here is not a question that preoccupies the beggars
along the streets in the Zona Rosa. The flower sellers
were deified by Diego Rivera but he only painted them
on their knees. They haven't yet learned to rise.

I buy a thousand faces of Frida Kahlo and a pet monkey
and wake up with white calla lilies instead of eyes.

River made of moonstone, of obsidian, of salt.
Mist with its small ivory noise.
The death of the sun: on this day the volcano will erupt
and the rain god ride down from the sky
on the coiled tails of rattlesnakes.

No, I'm not dreaming. My sisters and I are the four
directions of the compass, each one assigned a symbol
and a road to follow to the Temple of the Moon.

In the mirror the transvestite sees not his elegant
flowered dress or his scarlet nails, but his necklace
of tiny skulls interspersed with winged demons, too heavy
to fly. The face behind the face in the mirror
we confront.

As I was saying: here is this empty life. Fill it
with rain and flowers, a feathered coyote disguised

as a comet leaving a trail of hairless dogs
and chihuahuas to populate the Valley of Mexico.

When I was here at 25 it was like this: the middle of April,
jacaranda trees spilling purple blossoms
onto the sweaty shirts of shoeshine boys in the plaza.

Ahead of me in the crowd at the anthropology museum
I see that younger self. I place gold frogs in my ears
and it begins to rain. I refuse to pray
and the angels hear me.

We have found answers but are lost, looking
for the questions. *Is fuchsia?* A question Diego
might have asked Frida as they travelled
on a crowded bus with their arms full
of flowers and loaves of bread and little daggers
in the form of kisses.

Everything arrives too late except in the movies,
like a lover one wanted years ago who visits unexpectedly,
a little rumpled, with apologies and a good bottle of wine.

Across the night sky streak pencil-thin forks of lightning.
A girl is hit and struck dumb. Now not even the weather
is a safe topic.

January Dreams with Tamayo

I

Red horse, ribs showing, escapes a barn,
dashes headlong into a bleak landscape.
Perhaps it's early spring in alpine meadows—
Charles Wright opens his cabin door in Montana

or Wyoming, but here the horse bares its teeth, eyes bloodshot,
fleeing a fire or its own mad story.

II

Twins approach in horizontal striped skirts and bare breasts,
holding high above their heads a basket of fruit for the world.
Their arms stiffen. As one they gently lower the basket
onto the blistered grass and weep.

III

I become the dude
in a baseball cap with harmonica in hand, astride a bar stool.
Air is a symphony of small red diamonds.
My shirt strikes a high note and holds—

Fable of Pink

Missing the monarch's migration I settle for
    the spirit wasps buzzing
    in the newly discovered former kitchen

of the convent in Tzintzuntzan. Not to mention
    the ruby salamanders, likely an undescribed species,
    hidden for years in the water tank.

I'm thinking I might give up on the hit-and-run, the
    slot machine, the Niño Fantasma spray-painted on the overpass
    near Chapultepec Park.

I'm way past your death-age, Lorca
    but I could vanish any second now,
    my duende intact.

A piñata filled with live scorpions
    and my teeth, having cost half a fortune, depart one by one
    in great pain and solemnly in the Mexican dentist's chair.

In the gallery, three bronze hooded figures
    preside. A black angel revs up in a corner,
    stoked on cappuccino.

Moonlight radioactive, spilling from hundreds
    of Mexican moons, midnight coming on
    like a formal courtship, bowing and offering roses.

Air crimsons above the volcano, everything tilts
        and the church, up to its arches in black lava,
        begging the roughened hand of Malcolm Lowry.

Christmas morning in Aranza. The iridescent star
        hoisted on a flagpole signals baby Jesus
        —fable of pink, agony of yellow,

demystification of the beautiful barren hills, babies lifted up
        to be blessed by the Christmas bells
        strung across the narrow streets by the seashell church.

I've abandoned my perilous childhood, and you should yours,
        waiting up all night in case the few glimpses
        of fireflies might bring it back.

Michoacán

The Purépecha, recast as masons and fresco
restorers, pose high on wooden scaffolding
beneath the indigo dome of the cathedral.

Gathered in swirling golden robes, beings
with flowers bursting through their skulls
romp along the colonnades, just arrived

from the brush of Carrington. Do we want love
each and every day of our lives? You bet your ass.
Divest oneself of everything but.

The humans in this scene are slowly replaced by
otters, sphinxes, ghosts. The wave of the future.
Awakened at night because of the minotaur

stirring among the agave. The primitive being
beneath the primitive being, the miniature spaceship
launched from the new deck, the day in shambles.

≋

In my Sestina of the Virgen de Guadalupe
she's two feet tall in a pink satin gown in Extremadura,
but along the road to the Temple of the Sun
in the New World
she's grown to ten feet
and been bequeathed a moving sidewalk.

≋

Incendiary, your skirt, billowing in the offshore wind.
You dispense votive cards and little blue candles;
I dispense with my pagan ceremonies, my father's untimely death
scattered as the false orchid flowers in Morelia one cool morning
in December. Remember? You were there, at the

back of the crowd, gone into shadow.
Or hiding behind Cuauhtémoc
and eagles up high, etching wing tips against deafening blue.

There's a ladder to a window, a window
to the stars. One foot in the woods
and one on the threshold. I don't love you.

Altitudinal Essence

Everywhere we look in the spring world of Bogotá
purple lilies radiate pure altitudinal essence.
We regret to inform you that every museum and art gallery
is closed but the glow of Simón Bolívar's
last residence shines on and on, and paint-splattered
mannequins cast off from noisy demonstrations
are kicked further into the gutter by hundreds of bored
soldiers, smoking and hefting their machine guns.

So we take the funicular to Monserrate, slowly like a crab
climbing the bole of a steep and rocky tree, past the many
eucalyptus planted as settlers up the mountainside.
As Tatiana, five, leaps about, we gaze down
at the dissected and trisected city, seeking the textures
of parks, the botanical garden, and the single large lake. Gazing up:
a series of immense chemical-green plastic tarps protecting
the millions of flowers for export—at least an improvement
for the nostrils.

Later, rushing forward in crepuscular traffic to shake hands
with the silhouette of Don Q. slouched on his horse
plodding along the wall of the Biblioteca Nacional, I am
consumed among the hyacinth bottles and crimson swirls
of an Obregón mural. By day's end I'm one with
the white plaster feet protruding from stacked firewood:
art of the new Latin American century.

Angel Falls

—angels of the rain,
angels of the lightning

The fastest way to the bottom of the 979-metre-high Angel Falls
is to fly a monoplane
    straight down in a barnstorming feat
    worthy of its namesake, pilot Jimmie Angel.

Today I am in a small plane, same year
    same model. The wings shiver.
        We dive and bank into mist.
The falls are stupendous,
          Auyán-tepui thrilling.

Then the instruments go haywire.

              ≋

In a motorized canoe we approach
    the base of the falls through Churún Canyon.

Hundreds of angels
    plummet down, wings back,
swooping, then soaring.

    The current pulls us to the lip
      of a dark green whirlpool
where objects—trees, bits of boats—
    have been circling the black centre
        for years.

The angels settle in the nearby trees and watch.

      ≋

On an elegant patio outside an elegant Caracas house
     in a large cage
hunches a female howler monkey,
     brought as a baby from Angel Falls.

We hold hands through the bars,
     eat bananas.
Like two Fridas joined by arterial threads,
     we are inseparable.

≋

On his second trip Angel mired his plane in the marsh
at the top of the falls,

    had to climb down.

        This was 1937, after Conan Doyle's *The Lost World*
        but before Spielberg.

    For 33 years his plane sat, a lonely skeleton, gradually
        disintegrating.

        When we fly over it we are treated to a replica.

    This morning I feel like a replica of a human. Can walk,
        converse, am functional.

    The monkey needs other monkeys. What is it I need?

≋

Auyán-tepui:

First of all the weather is inhospitable
    unless you are amphibious.

Fogs, clouds, dew, mist—precipitation in all its forms,
    2-4 metres each year.

    Then the roar of the water, incessant daylong
        and through the damp, singular nights.

Each footstep can crush a threatened plant species, so squelch on
    on tiptoe.

≋

Ruth Robertson and co. set out in 1949 to record
    with theodolite the exact height of the falls.

    The Pemón who guide her
        stall at the Rio Churún's mouth,
            examine the portents.

They paint body and face red with vegetable dyes,
    chant their magical songs—

The whole expedition coming back as howler monkeys,
        pumas, pale-throated sloths, long-tailed weasels

in the next life,

    forgetting words, fitting into the sky.

Cosmological

Zapotecs

I would like to be kidnapped by a Zapotec
but am too small to climb the pyramids.

Learn to stuff the pavo in Náhuatl—domestication
of the braceleted fertility goddess took centuries.

Her tiny Oaxacan sandal is the destination
of all these raucous pilgrims.

The quiffed hair, the nose plug: this handsome
terracotta dignitary leaves me speechless.

Go visit the vampire bat, he's divine.
Carries our deaths through the endless night.

I rasp a stick across a turtle shell. The dark
belongs to me, and the horrible twilit blue.

Cuicuilco

In the Valley of Mexico the heat fears nothing and gathers in great clans.

Jade-faced and outmaneouvered, the Water Goddess stands
thin-lipped on the terrace, clenching and unclenching her fists.

At her feet, the coral snake coils, uncoils; the volcano begins to surge.
Her amber hibiscus wilts.
She'd like to be cool, translucent onyx,
to slip into the sacred springs and bathe,

but her many rooms are guarded by nightmares. Her astrologers
give special tours of the twelfth planet, carry home
fistfuls of its hair.

Falling Stars

Foremothers of the earliest gods: irritable, insomniac.
We have no temples, no spies,
no secret springs.
We each possess a limestone cave and a maize plant.
To the desperate moon
we write epics on fig-bark paper or deerskin
folded into screens.
We experiment, form the first humans from mud.
After the mud humans collapse, we visit Antares
and her attendant constellations. They outfit us with falling stars.
We long for chili peppers, jade hairpins,
foot massages.
The second batch of humans we carve of wood:
from the highlands, pine; oak from the ravines.
The square root of 3 is too much for them. They can neither count
nor swim. They haven't mastered the art of conversation.
For vanilla and turquoise beads
we'd shoot the moon.
A third group, baked but burned. Rotten to the core.
Annihilated by a deluge of night-coloured rain.

Cheek to cheek we dance with the ocellated turkey, we make salt
and honey, we create true humans of maize dough.
Add a few grains of XYZ, watch them rise.

Lethal Green

We gaze at our painted bodies in the cloudy
mirror, don the jaguar pelts, and gaze again.
Up and down our steaming limbs we rub palm oil,
rearrange our hundred vibrant feathers.
We treasure our ceremonial axes and decorative shields.
We envy no one.
The weight of no envy is dumbfounding.

Our rooms are crammed
with blue statuettes of the dead.
Cross-legged below the jaguar throne,
dwarves don't come when we call.
In our beds we hide werejaguar babies.
We don lethal green. For ships, for sails, we scan the horizon.
Our elongated foreheads grow chill with greed.

Three Rain Gods

Three Rain Gods afloat on a lake
in their divine canoe.
Of fish, a trinity too. A woven basket.
A send-up: the rumble, the cloud action.
They converse with other deities:
the Old Paddlers, the Young Maize God,
corn-silked and web-footed.
Setting themselves up as a koan.
Oh, she moans, don't be three, be singular.
Fracture the lonelyhearts light of March,
bleak and merciless, slippery.
The Rain Gods hate their job
but love to fish, all day, all night.
Dazzling in lapis lazuli wetsuits.
Deep in thought and speaking fish. With earplugs
and white shell goggles for seeing intercloud.

Cosmological

Either the royal blue flower is gigantic or
the god inside is quite petite. It's a he.
Wrinkled face, powerful body.
Metallic green bees come and go
with news of ball games.
Red Sox fans in the ditch, again? Overcome with anguish.
The gods of the underworld must have made a great trade.

He likes dwelling here, lulled to sleep
in his blue-sided hammock.
I don't. The walls are like a dollhouse mattress
or a soggy dyed-blue tennis ball
whacked back and forth by a pair
of hungover teenage girls
whose homework includes
the cosmological significance of zero.

Campeche

The wasp star, Venus, she's a witch.
She curls the snail in his house;
she's nine times wind.

Charles Olson is writing about the number nine
and all creation, while wind clack-clack-clacks
the palm fronds outside this ragged two-time village.
I'm five years old, visiting from Quebec.
Boys who have stunned with stones a frigate bird
now carry it up over their heads
and deposit it on the terraza.
How crimson its throat sac, suddenly puffed,
wingspan up to Charles's enormous shoulders,
eyes obsidian fragments.
Not bird eyes.
Little-girl-from-Quebec-who-yearns-to-fly eyes.

Songs for the Captain of Moonlight

Our beaten bark paper. Our monkey gods.
First feasting on quetzal tongues,
later singing rowdy songs
with the Captain of Moonlight.

The hieroglyphs on the propped-up stela shout:
Venutian! Lord of Smoke!
Listen to the dark clouds sing!

Graffiti on the fired bricks, hidden
beneath once-white stucco: an inebriated temple,
a tiny man astride a hummingbird.

And us on all fours, licking each other tenderly
like jet black jaguars.

People of the Left-Sided Hummingbird

Colours the Aztecs invented:
    eagle-devouring-snake black
        expansionist black
            black of the flowery wars
                dried-blood black.

    They loved the night creatures: owls, scorpions,
    bats, the Queen of Spiders.

    They prized a receptacle for flayed skin above all things.

    Roll back this black. What lies beneath?
    Blacker than a cave, the nine planes of the underworld
    at 2:00 AM, at 3:00 AM—

≋

Cell phone conversation overheard:
André got robbed in Mexico in some dirt hotel…

Well, the early houses of Tenochtitlan were dirt and thatch
(they had no hotels),
but the first pyramid was lofty, of wood and earth,

elevated enough for a life of terrible leisure among the sky gods.

: Sun, Thunder, Hail.
: Lightning, Stars, Galaxies.

Gods of fear, loathing, or distance. None belovèd.

≋

Climb to the top of the Red Temple,
covered with carnelian and soot black eyes.
Eyes horizontal, eyes vertical.
They glare, expecting tribute.

They are a one-way street,
like climbing a glazed wall with no rope
and the wrong kind of shoes.

If up to the next level you can pull yourself, straining and exhausted,
you will meet a single dark cliff, and a vast falling away.

Coming here alone is not recommended.

Choose a night when the moon
is raw silk. Focus while her indigo shadow
slides and glides slow-
ly across each temple wall, briefly closing one stone eye
after the other…

☰

Both Temples face east, where red originates, daily.

For breakfast you might be offered dog or turkey.

You could take a short walk to the Altar of the Frogs.
A rocky aspect would greet you,
the sound of wind in a high bare place.

I stand, bracing myself, in the middle
of the four directions of the world
and am torn to bits by desire.

☰

The water goddess has an aquamarine tail and a crimson face,
like you, my love. Like you.

The lives of common people (macehualtin)
were drops of oil on a heated pan: first sizzle,
then smoke.

Read the plan of the excavation of the Templo Mayor
by lightning. This, I find, focuses the mind
wonderfully.

≋

Behind the Aztecs, all night long, the feathered coyote
was licking his chops and howling,
leaping and soaring
every night, from the ascendancy of the Aztecs in 1430
until the arrival of the Spaniards.

Then he fled west, to the "place of women,"
taking with him the flowered trees
that hold up the washed-blue sky.

≋

Ehecatl, the god of wind,
invisible, indivisible,
whirls me away.

With him I consort,
become the pregnant spider monkey
who dances, tail held high in one hand,
as though with my partner.

All the while, scale after scale,
a snake, a dust devil, creeps up
my left leg, fangs flickering.

≋

As I write these words, past midnight,
a luna moth flutters against my window, ghost or hologram
of its black sister, antennae fine as fern leaves
unfurling softly against the glass.

Moon shines through its body like an x-ray.
Moon that's outpaced me all my days,
I beg you, don't desert me now.

    Blackest is abroad tonight
    and there are worse things than the obsidian moth,
    the star demons.

≋

Sometimes I have a greenstone heart.
Sometimes I am a sacred bat; I inhabit
the anteroom of the underworld.

≋

The Henry Moore bronze
    resembles a reclining chacmool
    on whose chest fresh hearts were laid.

But Henry Moore's is torn in half. So.

The pieces long to be reunited, but it's too late.

Before the Spaniards came, the chacmools were defaced,
pulled to the ground.

≋

And here's a little statue of myself, Tezcatlipoca,
the smoking mirror, one of four children
of the primordial creators.

I am everywhere!

Hard and brittle, I am the god
of war at night, of all actions seeking darkness:

theft
adultery
howling at the moon
assassination…

The Aztecs fashioned obsidian mirrors from the dark.
Whosoever peers in
sees my face reflected blackly,

so of course one's thoughts—a cloud of gnats
around one's head—are always bleak.

≋

Oh the divine spark of life! cries the hunchback
who will be sacrificed first,
when the sun battles the moon.

There is a big lack of events.
Days are too porous; nothing fills them.
Even the sky is inattentive.

Below me are carved conch shells and whirlpools
surrounded by ruffled feathers.

Auspicious or inauspicious is difficult to determine.

Blunted Gold

Dalí d'Hiver

A swizzle stick for your pensées
she said, handing around drinks,
tinkling of ice a little percussive,
the blue of the day too.
I've just seen *Spellbound*—

I'm rehearsing my dreams
for an interview with Salvador Dalí.

I zigzag across the graveyard one night
late in February, up to my knees in new snow.
He doesn't like interviews, but enjoys cognac.
I ask about a tear-stained clock, the many skulls
on loan to Georgia O'Keefe.

He draws near, finger to lips.
Listening intently, the lone tree leans in—
My Spain is blunted gold,
hot pregnant women in whitewashed rooms,
swallows carrying messages or flowers
from room to tiny room.

Far away, Lorca lifts a black umbrella,
weeps in a thunderstorm.
Red and jagged, my Spanish mountains,
brick-red as the roofs of Spanish houses tilted
precariously this way and that
on the wayward cliffs. When they tremble
I tremble.

The Clipped Language of Mathematics

I

Tom in printed shirt and black jeans defines, in the clipped language
of mathematics, the inverse of a matrix,

a forced translation of the life of a star. How I love you *alpha* and
beta, yes and even the square root of a window

where outside is blossoming the delirious magnolia
and crepe myrtle, the shy queen,

or a red-tailed hawk is dismembering a squirrel.
$N=1$ hawk a random sample so small we throw it away.

II

The boulder: russet, pitted—worn out by history.
A fragment of the moon, exhausted by lovers' laments,

witness to untold numbers of tired metaphors.
Beneath the boulder the woman with lavender hair

and violet eyes holds a pose for the sculptor.

Her calm demeanour, top of her class at Miss Elkington's charm
    school, but
boulder beats telephone book balanced on top of the head

for keeping the spine erect. In her mind she's hurtling through
outer space, no sign of gravity. Speaking to the stars in Arabic

and explaining the dreaded sum of squares,
the approximation of the approximation...

There are more than enough stars, like an audience, to satisfy
    sample size.

Signs of Water

With one crane fly and no sweetheart,
looking for signs of water
in the Martian hinterlands.
Rolling along the one-of-a-kind crater
without a care.
The crane fly all spindly legs,
like a hinged metre stick, graceless except when aloft
or resting its elegant tarsi on the spikes of fake grass.
Peaceful as a cemetery here. The holes in the sky
where the old moons lived grow blacker and blacker.
Day falls; night meanders,
its long legs trailing behind like lost kite strings.
The crane fly orbits me.
Probably my mother came here when she died.
I can't stop running through the talcum-powder-textured dust,
fiercely chanting the Kama Sutra.
The red mountains are scraping loose, heading for me
at the speed of glaciers.
In search of flight, I am shameless as the Wright brothers.
Lifeguards perch on high white chairs
atop the slowly moving mountains, waving flags.

Just Another Story About Billy the Kid

Through the ornate ceiling he shoots bullets.
The sky is very amber, sun indigo.
Puts his gun in his belt, whirls his peculiar hat
through the air.

Garter snakes shed their luminous skins
and one by one depart their communal den.

Night flies past. He puts his face
perpendicular to this century and weeps.
An explosion occurs behind a black door, then another.
When he sleeps he dreams of his former wives naked
in the dark, leaping from wildflower to wildflower.

He keeps lightning in a bottle, is stoked before evening.
Like a magnet he gathers action
and beautiful redheads, their frizzled hair
intertwined among the thunderheads.

In Bolivia Once

In Bolivia it took me five years to traverse a river.
Could be today I'm in a demolition derby or a boot camp,
my young lover about to turn 50, my serenity my anxiety.

Here's a toy dog, here's a little pool it laps—
with the moon and a forest scene including nearly nude
female, essence of beauty, incremental at best.

Same moon later on the darkened ridge, heaven needs editing.
In an old movie the moment's eclipsed and during the black-out
we're kissing like crazy, hiding from the director's assistant.

This month punishes my teeth. November, after the hawks
have migrated and the rock climbers descended
at sunrise, a bit stiff in the shoulders from holding up the stars.

Demise of the Flame Trees

Like flying machines: straw colour of linen wings,
soft balsam underbellies, elastic bands
keeping the tubercular propeller
from coughing up
    too much blood. At twilight.

    Aloft with moonlessness suddenly
    we behold a desert,
                where?

All the dry presences, hacking at something.

    Flame trees.

    Inside my mouth another mouth.

Fragrance of the Moon

Ghost of Buddy Bolden strolling Shell Beach, moonstruck,
scattering high silver cornet notes. Outscatting the moon.

Notes blown so pure and loud they create new tides—the now-famous
Bolden Tide carries away sleeping babies and old men

melancholic in their nursing homes.

≋

Fragrance of the moon:
white musk or cold, like new snow on granite. Leads

to drinking, dancing solitary at midnight. Oh, give me a kiss,
a honeydew, a spray can of *Moonlight on Demand*.

Those glow-in-the-dark stars I mailed to my nephew, belatedly,
for his birthday on the Ides of March, I saw them last night,

they made the Dog Star howl, they stole Cassiopeia's heart.

Comma Comma She Said
(Prelude to Mother's Day)

I

My mother's wrists descend redly;
her eyebrows are queen.

The magpie takes pleasure
in its blue throat of despair.

Paraglottis, epiglottis, glot, gloat—
don't let your tame stoat
steal my favourite reading glasses.

That's the way it's done on Mars,
it says so right in the manual.

Forgetting is recalling in some language.

Whatever happened to my mother's tongue?
It fell into a deep well and drowned.

II

The psychiatrist claimed she didn't have
a function. *To be is not a function,*

I said, narrowly, furious and filled with dread.

To err is not human. The bloodshot eye
of morning caws, casts its ever-loving light

on me. Let's go rob a Wells Fargo truck,
just you and me. We'll be back

in time for hot green tea. Time
to get horizontal, at one with the mosses

lying on their backs, no sentiment at all.
Weary, wearily, very, verily. My suit

is about to melt. It's made of duct tape,
your prom dress, uh oh.

III

Let's have a few zephyrs here, or Amelia's
ghost might visit, stay out there

in the ancient barn with all the
lovely horses, horses.

Red-cheeked Mongolian apples, do we
deserve the best? Yes, the best

money can buy. A sapphire, a burnt
rose. Petal love, petal love, be my

petal love. Sexual prowess is a
strange beast, usually comes lathered up.

IV

Your kisses do no good, even blown
by that mischievous breeze.

Kisses can't fix a broken door
so go get a hammer, some nails,

learn to speak inside out, begin
with the sound of yellow, it's

meant to be very soothing. Good
for interior decor—but pillows not drapes.

V

She seems very distracted. She's a
windswept meadow. Everywhere,

suddenly, her wildflowers bloom.
The rain begins with a tiny violet voice.

VI

Do serve me corn flan in an egg cup.
Don't get drunk on the cheek of a fish.
Say my mother never really left me.
Don't say her soul spread everywhere like jam.

If I choose to inhabit the Tahitian batik
don't tell me what the daughter of a suicide can't do.

If I fail my geology and metallurgy exams
don't remind me I'm the daughter of a mining engineer.

When the green is over, cruel winter,
bring me your twelve white hounds, ice kisses.

Would you love me better if I were a radish,
a rare dish, a white wine, a fine bouquet?

There is nothing like a blush
to encourage me to play *Red Pearl* on my zither.

Spanish Insane Asylum, 1941

By spoon or by force bright red food enters my mouth.
A black pig exits with an apple.
I feel prehistoric. Lindora, the nurse, insists it's a transitory phase.
What if my ears really do become arrestingly large leaves?

I think I will hire a pair of sculptors or brick masons
to carry me around in a closed litter today.
Tribal men in grey cloaks arrive and leave.
In the basement the double-headed serpent is training
to do figure eights.

In the middle of the arched bridge she halts
and lets her hair fall into the roiling water.
Each morning her three bluebottle flies attach to her wrists
and take her for a stroll.

Don't bother me. I'm painting tablecloths with meaningful symbols.
Erasing my father.
She gave me a set of pearls and then took them back.
She dresses me in tulle.

This ward is filled with quietly and noisily desperate souls.
In my left side there's an electric plug,
and my heart is lying by itself on a striped towel.
The resident squids spend their long days
reporting my every move.

Hanging over your head is a large pair of scissors.
When they should be sleeping, what do the townspeople of
    Santander do?
It's all the same, the storm principle.

The head on the back of the chair speaks to me.
Some days I prefer the darkness.

≋

Today the bison of Altamira thunder through the clinic.
We're near the sea, we inhale its rogue aroma night and day.
We're frightened by its suck and gurgle, treacherous depths.
I yearn for the burned-down 15th century town,
the stone buildings. Father Stone, I'll be yours tonight.

Can I return to Paris now,
to Mr. Birdman? Brilliant crimson feathers frame his face.
Is he mine or yours?
An elderly king in sapphire shoes is pulled along on a flat
horse-faced cart.
Is he going to the races or to hell?

She hides turkeys, smothered in gravy, beneath her bed.
I learn to speak owl.
There are many anorexics here but I'm not one of them.
He wants to be able to see through the wall
and inside my body to my uterus. It's ultramarine.

I'm a handsome man with too many secrets,
striding down a flight of stairs.
There's a family of cards in the room next to mine.
Queen of Hearts is the only one to speak. The others
moan and whistle, giggle and hum.

≋

...it's just my skin is not my skin anymore.
One attractive inmate keeps stroking my index finger.
If I concentrate hard enough I can disguise myself as a horse.
Or I could live the remainder of my life as a pogo stick.

The tide comes in and now they want to ship me to South Africa.
No, says the doctor. He wants to cram my veins
with yellow Jell-O.
My mind is alive with ghosts.
She puts slivers of mirror on my toast.

In my insect net I catch songs and voices. Of course
I don't listen to them!
She built a labyrinth in my room
so I cannot find my way out of bed.
All the inmates drink tea in the afternoons
out on the patio, with their nurses on leashes.

The priest tried to visit me but I saw the tiny devils all over his jacket.
His visiting card tasted of dark chocolate.
To reach our pills left on a sand bar
with our name on it, we all have to swim
in the dreaded ocean. I have the farthest to go.

Lip-Reading Jean Cocteau

I paint four horses, each a different hue.
I'm the one in the tree.

Hyenas in particular attract me.

Let me crawl out the window and into the graveyard.

Wear nothing but a sheet to the couturier's party
and drop it at some strategic moment.

Women dwell below ground, as pupae, as 17-year-old cicadas,
with bats, with strange night birds.

The topiary garden goes on forever.

She dangles two cigarettes, reads
Jean Cocteau.

With one pencil, one sheet of paper,
we commence tomorrow.

In the conservatory dwells the red-haired giantess.
She's in a night shift and so are you.

Fierce are the animals, with bright teeth.
They stand in enigmatic poses: here a shadow,
there a ripple on the nursery wall.

My fingers go inching around the room, measuring
everything in squares. Watch out! The hyena
will devour the chambermaid! I intend

to disturb identity. I serve a cannibal banquet: the skeleton
of a chicken upright on a platter, batting false eyelashes.
My father has a green head, green eyes; my mother

is scarlet. Yes, I'll sup on goat flambé and live white mice.

He clowns around for the photographer,
riding on her rocking horse.

I'm his lantern, I glow blue-green
in an icy scene. But my horse is frozen, my pointed
fitted boots don't grip. His hands are too smooth.

He's becoming a oiseau. My reflection vanishes in the mirror.

I arrive at Santander with my white horse.
We tread softly. I'm no match

for the woman in ram's head, corset, orange tights.
Nobody here has a mouth, just beaks and stubs of wings,
like ripped-off flower buds. They're hairy and furry.

My horse is a crime. They wear white masks.
Who owns the secrets of the insane?

When we reach Madrid, I will eliminate Hitler.
My father is Saturn, I am Moon.
I'm the bride of wind.

In radiography, a villainous room, I have two heads,
a birdcage where I abide.
The gates are sealed. Clang. Clang.
Only the egg has come to dine.

The Event

Here comes white death, the sly
thrill-seeker
shipwrecked,
    the barked dog
    thicker and richer and redder.

The event,
the golden syrup of it,
melancholy beauty, she's
    giving it all up: fan
    focus, brocade gown.

You could be my antitype, my other
other, genesis of ringed
things, foolhardy gumshoe
    locked in a cupboard.
    Strange embrace.

Zebra hidden in a striped zoo,
let your thoughts go
loose and slack.
    Make a run for it
    before the light stumbles.

Monkey Paws, Railway Ties

The walls were grey green and acutely ugly,
and scarlet of an unsurpassed loveliness.

The trains below rattled the walls. It was so serene
we could daydream.

Of rhinoceros horns and the evil eye, monkey paws
and railway ties.

There were no constellations; no constellations were there
anywhere in the Southern Hemisphere so enthused.

The chihuahua gods were stricken, epileptic, the clock disguised
as a dining table on a pair of blackbird legs.

We slept the day away on the bearskin rug. The walls
were serene. The train trembled so we couldn't even daydream.

Amazonia

Cametá

I recall the little town of Cametá,
how in the mornings the butter yellow walls of our room
would be radiant, light pouring in, farther in,
unstoppable. Then the mango trees wired with speakers
would crackle, daylong, Chico Buarque and English songs
from the 60s and 70s filled with saudade.

How do we survive the past, its long stutter
running beyond us as clouds fleeing overhead
on a windy day seen from the top of a hill. Then erase
one by one the hill, the wind, the clouds. One's private Chagall,
blue figure of dream, or the nightmare dragon with its
large malevolent eye, glistening in the cold rain.

Once I rowed a wooden boat
to a cobalt island, where all the rocks were shades
of blue. I dreamed this again and again.
Perhaps I was trying to grow up but could not,
for the blue was the blue of raw feelings, confusion, somehow
mixed in with my mother's sudden death.

South along the Tocantins
our last stop was Cametá, where we all nearly drowned
when the boat hit a partly submerged island, throwing us
overboard into the tall tangle of water plants, the black
turbulent water. Afterward, still in shock,
we ate a late dinner, telling the story over and over.

My mother's last Christmas, 1975, I was
the only child who didn't come, and I have always wished
I had been with her when they came to take her away,
and then carried her ashes to the graveyard in Toronto.

How calm the water looked, later,
as we walked by the untroubled shore, unable to sleep,
and the stars glittered hard and sharp, Orion
wheeling far away to the east—

Rumour of Silk

Tonight I should take the roan from the stables
and go, leave the old capital of San Salvador,

and my green-eyed beauty. She is wild, and longs for silk.
In the whole of southern Brazil, not a single silkworm.

Nor even a seed of a mulberry tree.
In the rainforest, it is said, everything grows.

I know the cannonball tree—its provocative crimson flowers,
and the ceiba with its secrets. The capoeira master

said I should travel north to Manaus. Where the two rivers meet
in ink blue and terracotta, I may find a rumour of silk.

The Suriname Frog

Above the city of Belém appears
an enormous silver fish. No one understands
its significance.

Every evening the black clouds coalesce
and spit blue lightning.

Sky God has a fin on his head,
pink eyebrows and very fierce teeth.

Higher than the moon vaults the Suriname frog,
photographs my face, tears the picture in four.

When I awake I have an amphibian air
and a curious sense of direction.

Sky God laughs, sends his harpy eagles
in pairs to hunt us. We are nothing but appetizers.

Uneasily, I paddle about in my weed-choked pool.
The frog has not overcome my fear of thunder
and cowers under the bed.

The Rainy Season

It is the red mud the perilous wooden bridges the parrots in pairs
the brazil nut trees the tapir the jaguar the rare orchids life on
the equator houses on stilts floating islands the handsome civil
engineer with whom I discuss malaria and the books of Eduardo
Galeano the purple-fringed passion flower the giant anaconda
naturally we are both married it is the full moon the extinct tribes
the rainy season the swarming black flies the vicissitudes of gold
mining the horror of Pinochet the assassination of Arbenz the
paramilitary in Colombia Botero's passionate paintings Guzman's
bronzes my pending departure his handlebar moustache the light
from southern stars

Belém

The first aphrodisiac I tried was from
    the Ver-o-Peso market—not
    eye of dolphin or the powdered genitalia
        of the giant river otter,
    but some herbal drink, bitter and nauseating.
        I was feverish, my face
        bland as a cloud.

        Nothing came of it.

    Later the same week
on a dare I ascended all the worn stone steps
of the Basilica de Nazaré, my head tilted
      to one side, whimsical, but something
        took my breath away.
        Something shone in the peacock sky
          and my breath was stolen.

        ≋

Nightwind in the jacaranda, the hiss
      of traffic along the avenida,
      a baker opening and closing his heavy
      oven door—

My mother sent me here from her deep dark places,
      sent me because she couldn't endure,
      old ghost, her story over in 1976, but
        I won't follow. I tip my straw hat
        to her, watch her dust
          settle in the mango trees.

        ≋

Thinking of the sculptor José Pinto, whose only record in Santarém
    is a bronze of a king vulture, 1927,
        that once stood atop the Teatro Vitória, since demolished,

I pick up my notebook
    and stroll with the Rio Tapajós,
    alongside a large white egret enthroned
        on a floating island of water plants,
    the creamy blooms nodding and bowing
        as they must have done
            when the last Brazilian Emperor Dom Pedro II
            sat for his portrait here in 1854.

Now the vulture resides on a black wooden table
    at the Centro Cultural João Fona,
        holding on, with pinched scaly feet,
    to a bronze replica of the world,
        where, for all I know, Dom Pedro still rules.

        ≋

I recall near Manaus an alligator
penned behind wooden slats in a foot of water, barely
    room for his plated body-plus-tail.
    I imagined each day his golden eyes
        sank a little lower.

A lone live chicken hanging from a stout stick
was lowered near his mouth.
    One lunge and the chicken was history,
    the stick in splinters.

A few feathers floated on the murky, oil-stained water.
The alligator hid himself, brooding,
his black heart and mine
a little blacker.

≋

Through the rivermist flocks of electric green parrots go
and the tide comes rushing in: big, bold, cold,
grey, in a hurry to arrive, in a hurry
to depart.

So the morning is summoned:
the little rose-pink shrimps gleam in their trays
in the open market.
On my silver tray I gleam too.

≋

One morning in February in the hot white rain,
alone in Praça Baptista Campos,
surrounded by the distant demeanour
of late 19th century English landscaping—the gazebos,
miniature bridges, everything so constrained
and diminished, at least to me,

I called upon the spirit Anhangá,
I huddled beneath the lone
brazil nut tree,

and a single blossom drifted down, turning
and turning—

≋

Life-size cardboard figures from the 1920s,
men in straw boaters, women in long swishing skirts,
stand outside As Docas on the grass,
    and the mauve flowers from the orchid trees
    fall silently, swiftly among them.

They follow us into the street, ask for our hats, our
    handkerchiefs.
    They stroll around the Teatro da Paz
      in yellow shoes
and look for everyone who's been lost.

Nights they wander through ruined houses
    and I travel with them,
        our neon eyes resting nowhere.

            ≋

Under the hot sapphire sky
    at the cool hem of the Atlantic,
    in 1616, the Portuguese arrived, in the name
      of their crown,
      wearing leather and metal,
    swords and helmets, and founded Belém. They arrived
        and kept on arriving…

Margaret Mee travelled here when I was four,
    her feet firmly planted
        in the footprints of Richard Spruce
        and Adolpho Ducke.

Now I stand overlooking the glinting water,
　　slick and moon-shot,
　　same nightwind at my back, same moon.

≋

I like to watch the jibóia take the sun
　　in the Emílio Goeldi Museum.
They have tree branches for props,
　　　　　a little grass, some dirt-brown murky water.
　　They don't do much. They are draped across each other
　　　　like much-chewed cigars, they never exercise.

　　Their stippled skin is amazing. It glides
　　　　　and sizzles under the bone white
　　　　　　glare of noon,
　　and the school children tire of it easily, but I don't.

I would wish for such skin, such muscle,
　　　　　so much careless grace.

I would see my old selves sloughed off as painlessly.
　　　　Goodbye to sweet Jan at two in sundress
　　　　　and little blue shoes, so long
　　　　　to the furious teenager who refused to rise
　　　　　　to any occasion.

≋

Even now the tiny chapel of the original Presidio São José,
  built, some say, on the blood and crushed skulls of
    the first prisoners,
smells of damp and old prayers,
but the immense glass wall makes a frame
    we look in on and go on looking in on,
      the paper cross high up on the far wall
      wavering in the slightest current.

The dreaded, cramped solitary cell is exactly as it was in
    the 1800s—
the curious can enter and leave at will—
      but when I stepped inside

    beneath the new fountain of white quartz
    fracturing water and light,
        singing tunelessly, tirelessly all to itself,
          beneath the fountain in the courtyard
      I could hear the old stones weeping.

                    ≋

I sit in the Parque da Residência, one leg
  crossed over the other,
  book in hand, in perfect imitation
        of the sculpture of Rui Barata, the poet.

    Side by side we contemplate the rouged lips of the orchids,
        glossy in the jambeiro trees, and the sky's
  azure bodice with its embroidery of pearl-white clouds,
      and I remember
a few days ago at the gold-mining camp in Palito,
  Robert's crew came off shift at 6:00 AM
        and saw a black onça sitting

in the red dust of the road
looking them up and down,

and later, pacing across the top of the great earth dam,
I wondered what large thing
might be looking me up and down
among the felted leaves and the singular
sun-bleached blossoms: cream,
then yellow, then cream again—

≋

Mid-afternoon in Santarém.
The equatorial sky has come to rest
on the twin towers of the Igreja Matriz, and now
their upturned faces have seen enough
so they close, gently but with a slight twist,
like morning glories
after the ecstasy of morning has passed.

Beyond them, the Tapajós slips its moorings,
casts off the shoreline, gives itself up
to the eastbound current. I too give myself up,
but it's not this current,
not this river—

July 2003.

At Ilha da Fazenda

The fazenda farmhouse tacked to the riverbank opposite.
    Last night the quarter moon rose, lifting it into the sky.

Plotting tribal wars or hegemony after midnight,
    the howler monkeys shout orders.

All morning the river rocks suck up heat
    through the jade green reeds.

Grateful for the summer clouds, the afternoon
    inside the afternoon, nodding in its blue sheets.

I kindle all day, building up my heat. By day's end
    I'm a torch. I quench my flames in riverwater.

Moon-splashed, the iguana nods in its tree,
    lightning puckers the rucked sky to the east.

Bats hustle insects in the afterglow,
    the oatmeal sand looses its heat, I loose mine.

Saturday night, stars shined up, Kid Abelha on the
    stereo, fish bones on the shore.

Yellow Dog

Nightlong in my dream
    a small dog, a yellow scrap, really,
        ran beside me, never tiring

I awoke in Santarém
    spent the morning along the river
        never tiring

I put out my hand for him to lick
    as anyone would
        little golden tongue unfurled

Never tiring, ran beside me,
    yellow scrap of a dog
        in my dream nightlong

Three Poems for the Rio Xingú

I

All day at the river's lip,
        looking out at the procession of grey rocks
        with bowed heads, gliding millennium by millennium
           out into the depths,

the heavy women, muscled Zuñiga sculptures
    climbing up out of the water,
        the washing in glinting metal tubs on their heads,

        basalt black hair like swallows' wings
        curved down their bronze backs.

At times what the eye can see
        the heart misses completely—so the emerald breast
        of a hill across the cobalt slash of the Xingú,

    shorn of its primary forest,
        is filled with the plaintive cries of grasses
          and the palms shine on
        in the glaze and dazzle of noon,

        the moon white cattle wade
          up to their thickened waists
           in the resinous light.

II

Late afternoon the iguana, its copper wings
    folded, ventures headfirst
    down the taperebá tree.

        I've seen its strange tracks all along the beach. It's heedless.

        I look over at the people by the river

    and am sure its days are numbered,
        as are mine. I lean back
into the palm's deep pool of darkness
        and begin to count—

III

Magellanic Cloud vamping in sequins tonight,
    Mars in its tall crimson hat. Both doubled
    in the black looking-glass of the river.

      Under the guava tree
in the shimmering air, creatures pass by and vanish:
        a pair of guinea fowl
        in best grey dress, a large turkey,

a restless, handsome chestnut horse, and then
    the night-pelt of the shy tapir
I'd been dreaming of. I arise and stroll
      partway with them,

beneath the saffron breath of the ipê trees,

· as the stars flow west, the river east,

and then dawn in its white scarves arrives.
I board a boat and am carried away
into another year.

Absolute Love

The Hydraulics of Rabbit

At fifteen I sketch RABBIT
not rabbit. Something
from nothing. Ink on thin paper, nearly translucent.
See lagomorph, see me.
Beneath rabbit's shadow, love is not
a many-splendoured thing but remote
and mathematical, dark blue in hue.
A hydraulics puzzle. The hind legs jacked up
on special levers, twitch of ears and nose the result
of many fine wires.

My father, water. My mother, on fire.
Scorching the door frame of the kitchen.
Jump little lagomorph, jump!
Into the convent, behind grey walls.
All those ominous watchers.
At the arched windows
the nuns wave goodbye, white
handkerchiefs billowing in a hot wind,
when I'm accepted into Real Academia.
The same wind, years later, chases me across the Atlantic.

Absolute Love

Because absolute love is not to be found
I settle for lesser loves. My personae
behind the walls, in the furniture.

> In the morning before the fog lifts I can be found
> at the entrance to a cavern or on a tightrope
> over an abyss. I wear my mother

as a silver brooch on an outer garment, my father
a blue flame at my throat. Everything I paint
is illuminated.

> I am adolescent, carried in the cocoon of my mother's
> flared cape. My sexual experience of Spain
> unfolds in brief vignettes. Suddenly I am naked

under a tree beside a cold mountain stream, a centaur
drinking the water. Afterwards
I expect miracles as some expect blows.

I Can't Identify to Species

Red sighs, oh, there were two at the edge
of the canvas.

I can't identify to species (because I invented)
the sinuous cinnamon-barked trees.
When I focus elsewhere they bend
nearly double. I am astounded by their antics.

Do you see the loop of love between my parents
in which I am enmeshed?
No wonder my hair stands on end.

Animated apples, lizards, clothespins
barter their way inside my sketch books.

Everyone here has a diploma, a nocturnal glint,
a trail of crescent moons from wrist to shoulder,
an elaborate hat. Everyone wakes up in the depths
of the night, nobody wants to play ball.

Pyrenees

Papa past midnight hunched at his drafting table
sending streaks of ink racing
across the immaculate white.

Water controlled and corseted by his dams
criss-crossing the Spanish countryside,
slate blue, sick at heart, seeking sea.

Trips to the Prado in Madrid I undertook
as a teenager to lunch gluttonously on Hieronymus Bosch
survive alongside dioramas of white-veiled
women in the marketplace at Tangier.

As though I were contemplating spending winter
in the Pyrenees
on my knees, as some might do.
Our Lady of the Mystical Rose.
Our Lady of the India Ink.

On the banks of the river Ter
I expect my parents to be reborn
along with bizarre scenes from Rua Indústria
in my hometown of Anglés
that seep sideways into my canvases.

One morning in Mexico City I awake painfully aware
I haven't the right gear for the Pyrenees.

Black Mask and El Greco

A skeleton in a bright cape strolls through the marketplace.
   Elegant in black mask and stripes
with his long fingers, he befriends El Greco

like I do, but centuries earlier. Who cares about time?
   El Greco, the ugly duckling, in his torn cloak,
enamoured of shadows, sketching by headlamp.

Too many Tuesdays in a row. White sky,
   white clouds, his bit of pink. Yesterday he was a navigator,
rudder in one hand, kite flying from the other.

The world has been created ten million times on spec.
   El Greco and I, we're closer now to the never-never
than at any other point in human history.

Golden

The bull, the sheep, the two white foxes

at the gates of the golden orange spiral city.

Sky dark as cherries.

Doors open, doors close.

Between one tree and the next, the bridge

sways with millions of leaf-cutting ants.

I bend down, catch snatches of dialogue.

On nearby islands trees float, ablaze with red buds.

Emboldened, in my yellow cape, I climb into a gondola. We circle

and circle the textured, sun-struck walls. Without enlightenment.
    Or rhapsody.

In the windows appear a lizard, two quarrelling spiders,

a luna moth preening in front of its mirror.

Spiral canals like nebulae, bursting with stars.

For this, broken-hearted, I have journeyed across mountains

and plains, across green surging seas.

My gondola tilts. When I regain my footing

I'm inside a glass globe filled with white flakes.

The galaxy is shaking.

Climatic

Indigo shutters carved with archaic symbols.

Behind them the weather is stirred, clouds materialize.

The alchemist envisions not transforming base metal to gold,
but ice storms to global cooling.

The meteorologist imagines she calves icebergs.

I stand in line to touch the wondrous New Age blue,
my exoskeleton in tatters, my many eyes iridescent.

The atmosphere, such as it is, is burning.

I hold the moon in one gloved hand, fall asleep
amidst the wreckage.

Delusional the razor's edge, the extra zero.

Oceans rising.

Seven Moons

On the brink of the escarpment
rise seven moons.

A woman peers skyward,
something startled written across her cheekbones.
Tenderness for the sky of midnight silk,
backdrop to the moons.

Far below, but travelling imperceptibly upward,
is a gaunt brown-robed man who identifies apocalypse.
A map tucked into his bag, his beard alight with fireflies.

Soon they'll share a fire and a grief.
She pities him. He is drawn like a scissors to her beauty.
His new theology does nothing to help her pass the night.

The stones and boulders scatter, a breeze
stirs his robe. He begins to boast
of water drums and food supplies.

Her vocabulary shrivels, her tousled hair flickers.
She sings a childhood song in a low voice
to praise the coming dawn. Moons
fade to nightmare. He promises.

In a Dry Place

Accompanied by coyotes and sidewinders,
  she wanders through a desert with a willow stick
  in hand.

The flamboyant ocotillo blossoms spontaneously ignite,
  then her ginger hair. She fingers lace agate,
  imagines herself in another place and time.

At her feet, mountains are indigo. She admires
  their solemnity, shushing the clouds parenthetically.
  All she needs now is to catch tuberculosis,

which she avoided throughout her catastrophic childhood.
  Then her year abroad will be complete.
  There hasn't been one oasis, nor desert palm,

nor amazing discovery of oil. She plays the shell game
  like the local officials with her passport and visa.
  Lucky she wasn't sold into slavery.

She doesn't speak the local dialect, any dialect.
  The desert ants are at her side as she sits, suddenly bone weary.
  They gather in the evening cool of her shadow.

Orinoco

In the dense forest, rainy season, in her snug skin boat,
with butterflies or leaves fluttering down from the low-slung clouds,
strange beings dwelling in the trees.

                                Her rudder a pleated fan,
                                her epaulettes.

Water-stained note in the pocket of the boat
—it might be the beginning of an era.
Cormorants dive-bomb a princess,

                                the air is prickly
                                with rouge rain drops.

Here's a view of the river's source: the sacred spring, and so on,
but the statuary's cracked, the frequency of earthquakes
turned up a notch.

                                Moonlight on still black water.
                                Nightbirds shuffling the leaves.

So far, not enough art in view, not enough vision.
The lady's orange hat is part of a tree! The large black birds
are speaking their minds!

                                No hibiscus tucked behind
                                her inner ear.

Her thinking black as the birds.
Suddenly she is inside the Palm House at Kew,
where moths wend their way

                                up and down the aisles.
                                Celestial noises,

a choir of armadillos. With operatic verve
the bat conductors flourish their starlit capes.
She steers among the trees,

> fingers brushing the leaves
> as though reading Braille.

Harmonium

Anyone's Desire

Desire, desire, desire! Give me back mine
    and I'll give you yours, or someone's.

Wrap your long hank of hair around Neptune
    and reel it in, cool ultramarine,
an immense astral fish.

Anything anyone wants, so do you. Radiant but
    spent, like nuclear fuel.
Watchmaker who doesn't know what time it is.

A whole street full of people carved,
    stepping off the curb from their brownstones.
Their hands ache, their feet ache.

Oh my adolescence, I sing, as I float westward,
    accompanied by a winged instrument.
Atoms go rollicking by on a conveyor belt.

Cheaper by the dozen, they shrill
    in high robotic voices. I think I am thrilled
but god is not, wails Flannery O'Connor,

her hair whipping about her face in the sudden
    desert winds. Her characters wail with her,
a long mobile wall, trailing off into space.

The lady in red lost her head. She strides
    between canyon walls, on perfumed tiles,
she glows at night. She's the real star.

Dressmaker

Whatever is left after the great conflagration,
will you be there? Will I?

In the dressmaker's shop all proceeds as usual:
the designer with scissors as eyes, the mannequin's chic dress
that doubles as an ironing board.

Their world does not allow for burning, heat prostration,
a deluge of cinders from Krakatau,

and anyway the shop itself is elevated, nearly
in the clouds, and everyone inside is so cool, debonair.
The air ripples with charged and coded conversation.

Whoever brushes by or is brushed by whom,
makes a killing in Madrid or Seville.

She is not standing on a decorative box to reach something forbidden
on an upper shelf. She is not covered with tattoos
of many tiny cobalt dogs sighing, leaping, rolling, begging.

Tower Song
(A Poem in Celebration of Darwin's Birthday)

I

She dwells alone in a medieval town, in the 21ˢᵗ century, how
is this possible? A stern-looking woman with a feather

tucked into the brim of her flat black hat. In front of her
an anonymous goateed man with a bulging sack of live birds

that escape one by one as he cycles along.
Behind her, young golden-haired girls in choir gowns,

more tentative, ride among the birds, pedalling
sedately but with rebellion in their hearts,

a jewel illuminating their secret desires. Away they go!
To the tower!

II

Somewhere outside time and mind,
the golden-haired beauties embroider the mantle of the world.

Some madman or genius conducts their weave
in time with high clear notes, a composition for flute such as Rampal

plays in the afterlife. They leap
into one of the boats sailing away on the

crystalline seas at the horizon—too many orange triangles
in the tower, and outside the sky is mutinous and unruly.

We see an animal (species unknown), a lobster, a nautilus wherein abide
three golden birds. The animals are docile and mild, for which we have

Mr. Blessed-are-the-Meek to thank. Evolution, we say, at the same time
someone insists on Lamarck's inherited musculature. It's akin to watching

a ping-pong match with an infinite number of balls in the air, or an
outmoded TV show we once sang along to, when we were much

younger, of course, but now we might be tempted again, if only to save
Darwin from such a ridiculous fate. *My* childhood, we shout,

stamping our feet.

III

One young woman flees to a new dimension, standing upright
with her arm linked to his in a boat made of thunderclouds,

lightning to steer by. She wasn't at ease in the tower,
wanting a different life, much improved, enchanted, constructed,

glorious, the weather not to be trifled with. The sky striated and hot,
despite the lateness of the hour, and he, cast from a heaven

in which we do not believe, conjures a sail from his linen cloak.
They are headed toward a mountain, whispering

because of what might be within hearing or firing range. After all,
they have run away and now they are shocked to see themselves

up ahead and from the back, but younger. Frightened,
determined, nothing can stop them. They enter the lit cave.

Eros

Handsome marble statue, fig-leafed, upright
on a pedestal in a fountain in a courtyard paved
with slate flagging and last year's leaves. Eros,
we guess, his irises gleaming emerald,

his torso taut as a drum. Beyond the courtyard
it's early spring, lilacs with their heady scent,
everywhere the luxury of novel, riotous growth.
I wonder what you are doing in Paris tonight,

and with whom. I wonder how we conjured a love
that became so swollen and discordant. Your borrowed
views of women, sweetheart, were positively archaic.
Don't ask how I'm doing because I've had a bad day

on the lip of a volcano, exploring the ruins of Cuicuilco
in the searing Mexican sun, the mysteries of Paracelsian
alchemy turning my brain into a knot.
There remain streets of blasted statuary

and rubble between us, my darling,
despite our shared history of surrealist art,
decalcomania and Freudian psychoanalysis.
Long past midnight Eros steps cautiously out of his pool

and approaches a door, knocking discreetly, meets
a striking dark-haired woman, doffs his fig leaf
and you can guess the rest, except he doesn't
return to the fountain or the century that created the courtyard.

Galaxies

It's long past the end of the 20th century
                        and the star catcher has been active
                    for decades

androgynous, in clothes tinted by deep seas
and new milk, trained in the subtle nuances
                        of human voice and gesture
                            —liquidambar eyes—

            climbing on and off continental trains
in the hours between 2:00 and 4:00 AM
—when there were such trains—

        or mingling with common folk in bars, munching tapas,
                    drinking fine bottles of Rioja
                        enjoying Gaudí
        as much as anyone

            peering in amongst the skulls and thigh bones
    in medieval ossuaries
                the better to comprehend the Black Death

all the while evading detection as "other"
                        despite the odd outfit
            —glittering titanium net in one hand
            platinum cage in the other—

hours spent in libraries
                poring over obscure star maps
                        memorizing arcana

keeping track of time by astrolabe, sextant, hourglass

        eyes overbright and too eager
so standing next to him in line
          late on a Friday one might wonder
at the pulse ticking quickly
in the slender wrist

       and not register her skin
     —pale lavender shot through with fine golden threads—

or, in a different light, burnished copper
        inset with thousands of glittering minerals

the better to see far inside the neighbouring galaxy
where the bounty per domesticated star
            is bound to exceed the value
        of the whole purpose of his life

      which by now has been abandoned
           to the gorgeousness of a star-free night
          overlooking a former planet

Rural Diorama

I'm fumbling around in some bushes that emanate a creamy
fragrance. I've an identical twin. Above the blue-tiled
roofs she drinks fresh coconut milk, she likes
to pour liquid chocolate over her arms and legs,

she's a sensation. Light bounces off the Portuguese
stones, these ruins. All the windows are high up,
as though in a prison or an asylum. We forage
along the steep slopes for olives, we read the *Hitchhiker's*

Guide, go out for lunch, then, too drunk to climb the hill,
sleep it off. What if my twin were a shooting star,
what if we run out of coins for the washing machine,
how about some luscious purple grapes with a blush

like frost on one side. The farmer would prefer
we re-enact our ancient rituals
elsewhere, so we'll just make a side trip,
take in Brueghel.

The One

The one whirring through a multicoloured haze,
perched on one of Leonardo's flying machines
with hundreds of metallic wheels and gears
underfoot, she might be in charge of the city of Paris,
her home-away-from-home atop the Eiffel Tower
in a summer thunderstorm, blazing hot,
sparks emanating from the wheels,
some centuries old, some newly minted, some
historic relics piked from a site in Burma or
Tibet. All the propellers keep time with the revolving moon,
so she waxes and wanes,
her glossy black hair emitting charges of light.

Glimpsed from a great distance, sans the
habitual lunettes (mes lunettes, ou sont mes lunettes?),
some (those Romantics) might perceive her as a seven-tiered
wedding cake, though untraditional,
no charming b&g figure nestled beneath a garland,
but with red and green blinking starboard and port,
a promise of rhapsody and high life, philosophy and art
over every meal.

Minotaur

Alluring, this minotaur, should you come upon her,
    blue-outfitted, holy-grailed, complete with long black key
in one hand. It's not easy to be brave without at least some totems,
    on sticks if need be, surrounding one on all sides

along with the extra dimensions required of string theory demanding
    labyrinthine mathematical structures for sustenance.
I sensed her once in our woods, near the wolf tree, and suddenly
    I was in full flight, down the path, beyond the meadow

and the two stately pines, veering around Rousseau's tiger that prowled
    among the sunflowers, oddly reassuring, helter-skelter
up the mountain, hugging the ridge, then pressed against the large
    cold flank of the moon. A very small woman, small as a ballet dancer

in a child's music box, gestured above my head, where was floating
    the keyhole in a grey dank fog and receding fast. Oh my anxiety,
my future, being lost in the midst, my middle age, flamingoes
    fleeing north, gods fleeing before them,

then the minotaur's shadow glimpsed once—so cool, with the key
    she'll never give over, her suave grey overcoat and enchantments.
How I desire to stroke her horns, her sensual pelt, pierce the fog
    any way I can— Give it up, I. Toss the key.

Imperial Cabinet

We could ship the spores by dogsled to his hut in the Himalayas where he cultivates them in an ingeniously constructed imperial cabinet, the humidity exactly as in a tree-fern forest.

We could say the heat is divine and mean it, despite the slickness of dampened streets where lovers kiss and part endlessly in black and white.

We would like to say that jeu mots are the thing this spring as opposed to, say, the gypsy skirt, the bolero jacket, the jaunty hat.

Where is the evidence for the exquisite flower in her phosphorescent hair? It was an orchid, we lifted it from a painting.

We are counting on you, now that the astral wind is slacking a bit in the rain-sacked palms and three tigers from the Cuernavaca Zoo are on the loose.

We would like to present you with a handmade marble fountain to recall for you the sound of running water, safe to drink, from your childhood.

Don't you agree some objects are seen more clearly on bended knee, craning the neck to peer up and around curves with the help of several mirrors and a bronze spyglass?

She thinks "still life," but doesn't particularly like pears or that famous flower arrangement with dead birds on the side, however beautifully reconstructed.

We could break the vicious circle with our wire cutters but the release of tension might bring an almost unendurable brightness. Perhaps we prefer to ride a little blind.

We wanted to inquire about the monotone, is it gone forever? Landed on the moon, then shrugged it off.

Iconographic

Encircled by stars, adrift, at dusk.

We encounter a woman in violet shoes bordered
with pearls who hoards inside them counterfeit cash.

At the same time a pile of salt accumulates underneath
our bed as though moles were digging industriously,
hell-bent on Tasmania.

An alligator skull above the door gives us pause.
It smokes a pipe encrusted
with rhinestones, seeks the invisible thread
that links every sentient being.

She muses on pentagrams, a chance encounter,
complex mathematical formulae that appear
across the sky after a storm in lieu of a rainbow.
No single self but multitudes, all squeezed into
the same body.

Birds return to roost at day's end like airborne
thoughts, knobby knees, scaly legs dangling.
Please notice my cologne. I ground it
myself from these ephemeral blossoms, aroma
of a passing shadow vaguely imprinted on memory,
shape of running antelope or wolf or star.

Where will these diaphanous wings
take my precocious double in her leaning tower?
How many planets are required to tip the balance
and beguile us with new plans, recycled bird-reptile
ancestors from the Age of Dinosaurs,

a whole host of primitive algae?
Up the tower stairs, around a corner
and into the cosmos. Melodious stars,
musical whip-scorpions, jug band

whooping it up at night, all night.
The sky vibrates with pulses of sound
and we are lit from within, battery-powered and scanned

within a centimetre of our lives. The yellow-jacketed
dust devil bows low over

a tendril of breeze, asks for our hand.

Postmodern

Women showcased in shimmering gowns
      and trailing lace capes—who's to pick up
the far ends, who's to know whether they glide
      into or out of the keyhole-shaped doorways
that might take us where we need to go next.
      He demands to know the context.

Turrets, a clash of cultures, the pterodactyl umbrella.
      The white machine has flywheels, gears, a dangling
string fixed at one end to a comet. It lifts water
      up and over a fountain, into a river valley,
down the road, past the hen house, and
      beyond childhood where even the evil dye

in maraschino cherries is now nearly forgiven.
      On the horizon—no, the horizon is missing
like a tumultuous stream that all at once
      drops underground,
out of sight and sound, rendering us mournful
      as those melancholic doves, my sweet one.

What shall we do without the excuse of running water
      to soothe so many of our flagrant violations
of form and function. The marriage of a checkerboard
      and an orange chest, an air-conditioner
and a copper watering can. Out this round window
      you might glimpse mythical figures galore.

They like it here, they can park like any car
    and hover for hours as clouds forming
and vaporizing, or as a mist over a river, even the one
    that vanished underground in an earlier stanza,
and now it's our job to lift any one of the fallen Stonehenge
    sarsens back up into its rightful place.

Harmonium

It begins with a retreat, a tiny bedroom with half-moon ceiling,
scarlet clouds rushing back and forth overhead,
    the room
swaying on top of an antique French commode
    complete
with handmade nails, accessible only by a string ladder
    which
at the moment is pulled up, no one home, at least not to us
voyeurs, trying to elicit some meaning, however trifling or
    inconsequential
from the placement of the house (not on a hill but on a plain),
    its cardinal
direction (facing west), the weather (deranged, unpredictable),
    stain
of the outer walls (undersea aquamarine) and so on.

Someone attempts to converse about his bleak times,
someone else composes on a combustible lute,
    fireworks
erupt in the doorway. Every drawer in every chest overflows with
    illogic
and passion, toy boat inside toy boat until the very
    smallest
sails away on an imaginary sea. The room is home to a former
celestial navigator, cosmonaut in the Russian sense, with
    stashes
of bittersweet chocolate, rubies, and complex iron
    keys
for the door to an adjoining room or the
    cell
of a prisoner unjustly held whom we are bound to liberate

if we can just broadcast her name loudly enough in a
sufficient number of nearly obsolete languages.
    Mongolia!
Send us your stalwart ponies and champion wrestlers,
    blaze
at us from your shining saddles, take a detour along the old
    silk
road and the eons will peel away like orange rind. You'll
be left with bounteous, edible but slightly careworn fruit,
    divisible
by eight and in harmony with all things that will come
    charging
out of the future, like a bullet train from Tokyo that gets
    derailed
on a steep curve, and, by the way, how is the creation of the new world

harmonics coming along? Beleaguered between treble and bass,
all the chords run riot in the streets.

Notes

AHORA
For Petra Fischer and Enrique Mendoza Morales.
Casuarina is the genus of pine that has been introduced into much
of Latin America, originally from Australia and the Pacific Islands.
It is rather delicate and wispy-looking for a conifer but it is a useful
windbreak. The kinkajou (*Potos flavus*) is a tan, nocturnal tree-dwelling
mammal generally found in the rainforest of Central and South America.
It feeds primarily on fruit and has a prehensile tail. Xochicalco, founded
before 700 AD in Morelos state (about 40 km from Cuernavaca) was
an important regional centre with many influences including Maya,
Teotihuacán, Zapotec, Mixtec, and Veracruz. The Temple of the
Feathered Serpent is considered its most striking structure. Dorothy
Brett (1883-1977) was an American artist and photographer born in
London, England, who was friends with DH Lawrence and his wife
Frieda. Cantera is a beautiful volcanic stone used extensively in carving
and building. The tule tree (*Taxodium mucronatum*) is a cypress found
in Santa María del Tule, near Oaxaca, Mexico. It is one of the oldest
trees in the world (possibly 2000 years) and has a circumference of 36 m
and is 11 m tall. Some local Zapotec people believe it was planted 1400
years ago by a priest of the god of wind, Ehecatl. The following paintings
provided a starting point: *Ciudad de Oaxaca*, 1795, Anónimo; *Del
Porfirismo a la Revolución*, 1957-1966, David Alfaro Siqueiros (mural
at the Castillo de Chapultepec in Mexico City); *The Architect* (Jesús T.
Acevedo), 1915, Diego Rivera; *La travesía*, 1935, Remedios Varo; *Nuestra
Vida*, 1991, Rodolfo Morales; and *Códice del Sol*, 1992, Maximino Javier.

THE FLOWER CARRIERS
For my sister Diane Conn.

JANUARY DREAMS WITH TAMAYO
Rufino Tamayo (1899-1991). Outstanding Mexican painter and sculptor.

FABLE OF PINK
For Carolyn Smart.
The three bronze figures are *Cuculati I, II, III* by Leonora Carrington,
a British-born surrealist painter and sculptor who lives in Mexico.

MICHOACÁN
For Josefina and Faustos Lara.
The Purépecha people flourished from 1100 to 1530 AD. Their main centre was Tzintzuntzan, near Lake Pátzcuaro in Michoacán state, Mexico. Cuauhtémoc was the last Aztec emperor. He surrendered Tenochtitlan (now Mexico City) to Cortés in 1521.

ALTITUDINAL ESSENCE
For Helena Brochero.
Alejandro Obregón (1920-1992). Colombian painter.

ANGEL FALLS
For Richard Summerbell and Ross Fraser.
The passage in italics at the beginning is by Hugo Claus, in *Landscape with Rowers: Poetry from the Netherlands*, translated and introduced by J. M. Coetzee (2004), Princeton University Press. Auyán-tepui is the name of the sandstone mountain (or inselberg) atop the Guyana Shield in southern Venezuela where Angel Falls is located. The Pemón people call it Kerepaküpai Merú (the deepest place). New World monkey (including genus *Alouatta*, howler monkey) and human lineages diverged approximately 33 million years ago. In 1949, American journalist Ruth Robertson led the first successful expedition up the Churún Canyon to the base of Angel Falls. The Tepui ecoregion (where Angel Falls is located) includes many endemic species of flora and fauna, some of which are endangered.

ZAPOTECS
The Zapotecs were strongly influenced by Olmec culture and traditions. They were known for monumental architectural works and complex ceramic urns. According to legend, before falling to earth near their centre, Monte Albán, in Oaxaca State, they were songbirds of many brilliant hues. In Spanish, *pavo* is turkey, one of only two animals domesticated by the Mesoamericans. The other is dog.

CUICUILCO
Around 100 or 300-400 AD (sources vary) the volcano Xictli destroyed the regional centre Cuicuilco in the Valley of Mexico.

FALLING STARS

This poem began after reading *Popul Vuh*, epic of the K'iche Maya, Early Classic Period. The ocellated turkey (*Agriocharis ocellata*) is remarkably striking, having a bright blue head with decorative red tubercles. It is found only in Mexico and Central America.

LETHAL GREEN

For Juan Nuñez-Fárfan and Sonia Careaga.

Werejaguars had human faces and jaguar mouths, and are characteristic of Olmec motifs, many of which were borrowed and modified by the Maya. Art that influenced the poem: beaker with ceremonial scene, Usumacinta Valley, Tabasco; ceramic painted plate, Campeche coast; Chama vessel, Chama, Guatemala; seated dignitary, Jaina Island, Campeche. All Late Classic Maya.

THREE RAIN GODS

A central image for this poem was "Three Chaks (Rain Gods) are catching fish," incised bone from the Temple I tomb, Tik'al, Guatemala.

COSMOLOGICAL

This poem refers to a ceramic anthropomorphic figure emerging from blue *Philodrendon*. Classic Maya.

CAMPECHE

For R.T.

SONGS FOR THE CAPTAIN OF MOONLIGHT

Ceramic bricks with incisions or modeling. Comalcalco, Mexico, AD 600-800. Maya.

PEOPLE OF THE LEFT-SIDED HUMMINGBIRD

For Mace Neufeld.

The Aztec patron deity is Huitzilopochtli (left-sided hummingbird).

THE CLIPPED LANGUAGE OF MATHEMATICS

For Christine Kowal Post.

The phrase "the clipped language of mathematics" is from T. Kepler, a mathematical biologist in the Department of Statistics at North Carolina State who taught at the Summer Institute in Statistics at North Carolina State in the summer of 2000. The sculpture referred to in section II is *Boulder*, 1999, by Christine Kowal Post.

COMMA COMMA SHE SAID.
For Oriole Farb Feshbach and Terry Allen.

THE EVENT
For LEM.

MONKEY PAWS, RAILWAY TIES
For Carolyn O'Neill and Michael Harris.
After Jay Hopler.

SPANISH INSANE ASYLUM, 1941
For Marlene Belfort.

LIP-READING JEAN COCTEAU
For Douglas Burnet Smith.
The line "*I'm the bride of wind*" is derived from the title *Leyendas del la Novia del Viento* by L. Andrade (see selected sources). Both "Spanish Insane Asylum, 1941", and "Lip-Reading Jean Cocteau" were inspired in part by the life and paintings of Leonora Carrington.

THE SURINAME FROG
The harpy eagle (*Harpia harpyja*) is a very large (over a metre in height) double-crested black-and-white eagle found in Neotropical forests. It hunts mainly monkeys and sloths and is now rare.

BELÉM
For Pedro Hernández-Abad.
Ver-o-Peso (literally See–the-Weight) is a famous market around the docks of Belém, established in the 16th century. Traditional Amazonian products can be purchased here, including an amazing array of medicinal plants and herbs. Anhangá is a forest spirit that protects all living things in the Amazon and is depicted most often as a stag. In Belém, The Docks, As Docas, along the Baía do Guajará, have been recently restored. The neoclassical Teatro da Paz was built in 1874. Margaret Mee (1909-1988) was an outstanding botanical illustrator and naturalist who for many years worked and travelled in Amazonian Brazil. Richard Spruce, the British botanist and explorer, spent years (1849-1864) navigating and collecting along the Amazon, describing scientifically for the first time hundreds of previously unnamed botanical specimens. Adolpho Ducke (1876-1959) was a highly regarded

Brazilian entomologist, ethnographer and botanist who worked primarily in the Amazon. Jibóia is the common name for the boa constrictor (*Boa constrictor*). Tan, with a diamond-pattern of darker brown, it is relatively common in Brazil, but, being nocturnal, is rarely spotted by most visitors to the Amazon. Rui Barata was a modern Brazilian poet. The tree commonly known as jambeiro (*Eugenia jambos*) is from Asia, but was imported into the Amazon basin. It has exceptionally beautiful fuchsia flowers and red edible fruit. Onça is Portuguese for jaguar (*Panthera onca*). These predators are both feared and revered by some indigenous people, but unfortunately, despite being endangered, they are also hunted ruthlessly for the international fur trade.

ILHA DA FAZENDA
Kid Abelha is the name of a contemporary Brazilian pop band.

THREE POEMS FOR THE RIO XINGÚ
For Goreti (Maria Goreti Rosa-Freitas).
Francisco Zuñiga (1912-1998) was a Costa Rican painter and sculptor who made his name and reputation in Mexico. Taperebá is the common name of the tree *Spondius mombin*, often abundant in secondary forests. Its seeds and plum-like fruit are important dietary components of some neotropical primates. Ipê, found throughout Brazil, is the common name for the yellow-flowering canopy tree *Tabebuia serratifolia*.

A NOTE ON REMEDIOS VARO
The poems in the last two sections, Absolute Love and Harmonium, were inspired by the paintings and texts of Remedios Varo (1908-1963), a member of the surrealist school whose work reflects a unique interior vision, a fabulous blend of mythology, alchemy and science. She was born in Spain and was from an early age trained in drafting by her father, a hydraulics engineer. She attended the prestigious Real Academia in Madrid, lived in Barcelona, then Paris. She married the surrealist poet Benjamin Péret. Threatened after the Nazi invasion of France, as were many leftist artists and intellectuals, they fled to Mexico by boat. After many struggles, Péret returned to France. Varo remained for the rest of her life in Mexico where she produced her most memorable work.

DRESSMAKER

Krakatau is a volcano on the island of Rakata between Java and Sumatra. It has a long history of seismic activity, erupting most recently and famously in 1883, when two-thirds of the island was destroyed and record-breaking tsunamis killed at least 36,000 people.

GALAXIES

Liquidambar is a genus of tree, found in Asia and North America. One species, *L. styraciflua*, is commonly known in North America as sweet gum or red gum.

Selected Sources

Alberth S. L. 2004. *Leonora Carrington: Surrealism, Alchemy and Art.* Lund Humphries Ltd., Hampshire, UK and Burlington, VT.

Lourdes A. 2001. *Leyendas de la Novia del Viento.* Libros de la Espiral, Artes de Mexico, Mexico, D.F.

"Arqueología Mexicana." 1995. *Olmecs.* Special Edition. Editorial Raíces/Instituto Nacional de Antropología e Historia, Mexico.

"Artes de México." 2003. *México en el Surrealismo: Los Visitantes Fugaces.* Número 63.

Basilio M., Bercht F., Cullen D., Garrels G., Pérez-Oramas L. E. 2004. *Latin American & Caribbean Art MoMA at El Museo.* El Museo del Barrio and The Museum of Modern Art, New York.

Braum B. 2000. *Pre-Columbian Art and the Post-Columbian World.* Harry N. Abrams, Inc. New York.

Carrington L., Weisz E., Weisz Carrington G., Weisz Carrington P. 2005. *Universo de Familia.* Museo del Palacio de Bellas Artes, Impronta Editores, S.A.

Chadwick W. 2002. *Women Artists and the Surrealist Movement.* Thames & Hudson, Inc. New York.

Coe M. D. 1999. *The Maya.* 6th Ed. Thames & Hudson, Inc. New York.

Galeano E. 1982. *Memoria del Fuego. I. Los Nacimientos.* Siglo Veintiuno Editores, S.A.

Governo do Estado do Pará. 2004. *Belém da Saudade. A Memória da Belém do Início do Século em Cartões-Postais.* 3ª edição. Secreteria Executiva de Cultura, Belém, Pará, Brazil.

Kaplan J. A. 2000. *Remedios Varo: Unexpected Journeys.* Abbeville Press Publishers, New York & London.

Kricher J. C. 1989. *A Neotropical Companion. An Introduction to the Animals, Plants, and Ecosystems of the New World Tropics.* Princeton Univ. Press, NJ.

Levitt H. 1997. *Mexico City.* Doubletake & W.W. Norton & Co., New York, London.

Longhena M. 1998. *Splendours of Ancient Mexico.* Thames & Hudson, London.

131

Lozano L-M. 2000. *The Magic of Remedios Varo*. National Museum of Women in the Arts. Schmitz Press, Sparks, MD.

Markman R. H., Markman P. T. 1994. *Masks of the Spirit*. U. California Press, Berkeley, CA.

Matos Moctezuma G., Solis Olguin F. 2002. *Aztecs*. Royal Academy of Arts, London.

Miller M., Martin S. 2004. *Courtly Art of the Ancient Maya*. Thames & Hudson, New York.

Olson C. 1965. "Mayan Letters" in *Selected Writings*, Ed. Creeley R. New Directions Books, New York.

Rivera M. 2005. *Trampantojos. El círculo en la obra de Remedios Varo*. Siglo xxi Editores, Argentina, S.A.

Rothenberg J. 1969. *Technicians of the Sacred*. Doubleday & Co., New York.

Shoumatoff A. 1986. *In Southern Light*. Hutchinson Ltd., London, Melbourne, Auckland, Johannesberg.

Solis F., Leyenaar T. 2002. *Mexico – Journey to the Land of the Gods – Art Treasures from Mexico*. Waanders Publishers, Amsterdam.

Spruce R. 1908. *Notes of a Botanist on the Amazon & Andes*. Ed. Wallace, A.F. Macmillan and Co. Ltd., London. Vol. I and II.

Sullivan R. 1996. "P.K. Page in Mexico." *Brick*, No. 55. pp. 25-30, Toronto.

Varo R. 1997. *Cartas, sueños y otros textos*. Introducción y Notas de I. Castells. Ediciones Era, México, D.F.

Varo R. 2002. *Catalogue Raisonné*. Third Edition. Ediciones Era, México, D.F.

Acknowledgements

Grateful acknowledgment is made to the editors of those publications in which the following poems originally appeared:

The Antigonish Review: "The Suriname Frog," "Signs of Water," "Demise of the Flame Trees," "Campeche," "Cosmological," "Cuicuilco," "Songs for the Captain of Moonlight" (as "Our Monkey Gods")
Arc: "Ahora"
Bei Mei Feng: "I Can't Identify to Species"
Barrow Street: "Three Rain Gods"
CV2: "Zapotecs," "Absolute Love," "Dressmaker"
enRoute Magazine: "Belém," "At Ilha da Fazenda," "Three Poems for the Rio Xingú," "Yellow Dog"
Event: "Angel Falls"
The Fiddlehead: "The Rainy Season," "Comma Comma She Said," "Lethal Green," "Michoacán," "In a Dry Place"
The Fieldstone Review: "Just Another Story About Billy the Kid"
The Literary Review of Canada: "Minotaur"
The Malahat Review: "In Bolivia Once," "Golden," "Orinoco"
The Massachusetts Review: "The Flower Carriers," "Cametá"
Prairie Fire: "Fable of Pink," "Harmonium"
PRISM international: "Rumour of Silk" (as "Leaving San Salvador"), "Fragrance of the Moon," "The Clipped Language of Mathematics," "Lip-Reading Jean Cocteau," "January Dreams with Tamayo"
Room of One's Own: "Falling Stars"
Vallum: "Dalí d'Hiver"

Amazonia, a group of poems, comprised of "Belém," "At Ilha da Fazenda," "Yellow Dog," and "Three Poems for the Rio Xingú," won second prize for poetry in the CBC Literary Awards, 2003. Some of these poems were broadcast on CBC Radio One's *Between the Covers*, *The Arts Today*, and on *Richardson's Round-up* during the spring of 2004. "Belém" is one of the Vehicule Press Virtual Chapbook online series (since 2005). "Golden" won the *Malahat Review's* 2006 inaugural P.K. Page Founders' Award for Poetry. "Galaxies" was on the *Poem of the Week* Parliamentary Poet Laureate's website (www.parl.gc.ca/poet), 2007-2009. Some of these poems were broadcast on CHSR, Fredericton, New Brunswick, and on CKDU, Dalhousie, Halifax, Nova Scotia, in March, 2007. "Iconographic" was published in a limited edition chapbook,

Common Magic: The Book of the New, ed. E. Greene and D. Gugler, Artful Codger Press, Kingston, Ontario, 2008. Some poems were broadcast in March, 2008 by CFRC at Queen's University, Kingston, Ontario, in conjunction with Common Magic, a celebration of the life and work of Bronwen Wallace. Several poems were broadcast on WGLT Poetry Radio, Illinois State University, Normal, Illinois in the spring of 2009. Several poems were included in *How the Light Gets In: An Anthology of Contemporary Poetry from Canada*, ed. J. Innis, Waterford Institute of Technology, Ireland, 2009.

For insightful editorial commentary I am grateful to David Conn, Diane Conn, Jane Southwell Munro, Carl Schlichting, and Carolyn Smart. I am happy to acknowledge the eyes and ears of the members of the Amherst Poetry Seminar. Long may we meet! Special thanks to Christine Kowal Post for introducing me to her powerful and playful sculptures. Juan Nuñez-Fárfan and Sonia Careaga provided warmth, hospitality and friendship during many trips to Mexico City. For an annual haven in Belém where many of the Brazilian poems were originally conceived, I am deeply grateful to my scientific collaborator and exceptionally gifted and resourceful friend, Marinete M. Póvoa, and her family. I thank Simon Dardick and Nancy Marielli for supporting my work through thick and thin, and for choosing "Belém" for their Virtual Chapbook online series. I am honoured to use the glorious painting, *México en negro*, by Leslie Zeidenweber, for the cover. I also thank Leslie and her husband Jaime Venguer for their support and inspiration, and for the marvelous atmosphere they provide during visits to Mexico City. Great thanks to Stan Dragland at Brick Books for editorial discussions and enthusiasm, and for a multi-faceted friendship. Kitty Lewis, as always, provided tremendous help and advice. I am grateful to Alayna Munce for her fine copy-editing skills. Alan Siu made a fantastic painting into an even more fantastic cover.

Jan Conn was born and grew up in Asbestos, Quebec and has since lived in Montreal, Vancouver, Toronto, Guatemala, Venezuela, Florida, and Vermont. She now lives in Great Barrington, Massachusetts. She has published six previous books of poetry, most recently *Jaguar Rain, the Margaret Mee poems* (Brick Books, 2006). Her poems have appeared in many literary journals and anthologies and a selection of Amazonian poems won second prize in the CBC literary awards, 2003. She won the inaugural (2006) P.K. Page Founders' Award for poetry. For more information see www.janconn.com. She received her Ph.D. in Genetics from the University of Toronto in 1987 and is a Research Scientist at the Wadsworth Center, New York State Department of Health, and Professor in the Department of Biomedical Sciences at the School of Public Health at SUNY-Albany. Her research focuses on the evolution and ecology of mosquitoes that transmit human pathogens, especially malaria parasites. Fieldwork takes her frequently to Latin America.